BRETT
FAVRE

*(Photo on
front cover)*

*(Photo on
previous pages)*

**Brett Favre looks
to throw during
Super Bowl XXXI
against the New
England Patriots.**

**Favre unloads a
pass late in the
game against
the Tampa Bay
Buccaneers.
Green Bay went
on to win 34–3.**

Library of Congress Cataloging-in-Publication Data
Rambeck, Richard.
Brett Favre/ by Richard Rambeck.
p. cm.
Summary: Presents a biography of the quarterback who led
the Green Bay Packers to victory in Super Bowl XXXI.
ISBN 1-56766-458-X (lib. bdg.)

1. Favre, Brett-Juvenile literature. 2. Football players—
United States—Biography—Juvenile literature. 3. Green
Bay Packers (Football team)—History—Juvenile literature.
4. Quarterback (Football)—Juvenile literature. [1. Favre,
Brett. 2. football players.] I. Title.
GV939.F29R36 1997   97-11613
796.332'092—dc21   CIP
[B]   AC

BRETT
FAVRE

BY RICHARD RAMBECK

As Brett Favre walked to the line of scrimmage, he looked over the New England defense. Right away, Favre knew that the play called in the huddle should be changed. The play was a short, safe pass. The Green Bay coaches knew that Favre often struggled at the beginning of games. They wanted their quarterback to gain confidence by completing his first pass in Super Bowl XXXI. But the New England defense was expecting the short pass. The Patriots had both their safeties near the line. Favre knew his receivers could outrun the New England safeties.

At the line of scrimmage, the Green Bay 46, Favre called another play, a long pass. "I told Brett that if he wants to change the play, that's fine, but it better work," said Green Bay Coach Mike Holmgren. "It worked beautifully." Yes, it did. As Favre dropped back to pass, Packer receiver Andre Rison ran right by his defender. Favre threw a perfect pass that hit Rison in stride for a 54-yard touchdown. When Rison scored, Favre tore off his helmet and raced around the field, holding the helmet high over his head. The Packers had a touchdown on only their second play of the game.

Before Super Bowl XXXI started, Favre was a nervous wreck. He had also been sick. Three days before the game, he was in bed with a fever of 101 degrees. "I was worried," said Favre, who pronounces his name as if it were spelled "Farve". "I'd waited my whole life to play in this game, and now I wasn't going to be healthy." He felt much better however a couple of days later. Except for a case of nerves, he was fine when the game started. This was, after all, the game he had been telling people for months he was going to play in and win.

Favre fires downfield, with blocking protection from guard Adam Timmerman, against the Carolina Panthers in the NFC Championship Game.

*Favre searches for a
receiver during the
first quarter in a game
against the Kansas
City Chiefs.*

In July, before the season even started, Favre said, " I'm going to win the Super Bowl. And if you don't believe me, bet against me. You'll lose." Half a year later, Favre was living up to his promise. His touchdown pass to Rison gave the Packers a 7–0 lead over New England. Green Bay then stretched the lead to 10–0 on a Chris Jacke field goal. At that point, Patriot quarterback Drew Bledsoe got hot, and the New England defense started to shut down the Packers. Bledsoe drove the Patriots to two touchdowns before the end of the first quarter, giving New England a 14–10 lead.

Suddenly it appeared as if the Packers were in trouble. They were supposed to win this game easily. But they were behind, and their offense wasn't going anywhere. Favre had every reason to be nervous now, but he wasn't. He knew Green Bay could move the ball against New England. Early in the second quarter, the

Packers had the ball on their own 19-yard line. Favre looked over the New England defense and saw that Patriot safety Lawyer Milloy was man-to-man with Green Bay receiver Antonio Freeman. The play called in the huddle was a short pass, but Favre had a better idea.

At the line of scrimmage, Favre changed the play. He sent Freeman deep and hit him with another perfect pass. Freeman outran Milloy and the rest of the Patriots for an 81-yard touchdown. It was the longest pass play in Super Bowl history. It also gave the Packers a 17–14 lead. Green Bay would not trail again. Later in the second quarter, with the Packers ahead 20–14, Favre drove his team down the field. From the New England 2-yard line, Favre rolled out to the left. His receivers were covered, so Favre started sprinting for the end zone. Just before he went out of bounds, he stretched the ball across the goal line.

Favre throws a shuffle pass to running back Dorsey Levens against the Minnesota Vikings.

Favre's touchdown gave the Packers a 27–14 lead. They went on to win Super Bowl XXXI, by a score of 35–21, just as Brett Favre had told everyone back in July. After the game, Packer kickoff and punt returner Desmond Howard came up to Favre. Howard, who scored the game's last TD on a 99-yard kickoff return, was named the game's Most Valuable Player. But Howard knew who had been the team's MVP all season long. "You really deserve this," Howard said to Favre. "You deserve to be a Super Bowl winner." Favre smiled and hugged Howard.

For a while during the 1994 season, it wasn't clear whether Favre deserved to be Green Bay's starting quarterback. After a loss to Minnesota, Coach Mike Holmgren was considering whether to bench Favre and start Mark Brunell. In fact, most of the Packer players felt the team should change quarterbacks. They knew Favre was talented, but they felt he made too many mistakes. In 38 games as a starter for Green Bay, Favre had thrown 46 touchdown passes — but also 44 interceptions. At that point, the Packers were a good team, not a great one.

Holmgren wanted a quarterback who could lead Green Bay to the Super Bowl. Frankly, he wasn't sure Favre could do that. But Holmgren took a chance. He called Favre into his office. "Buddy," Holmgren said to Favre, "it's your job." Favre had worried that Holmgren lacked confidence in him. Now, the quarterback knew his coach was ready to put the team's future in his hands. "The second half of the season is going to be like no other," he promised Holmgren. Favre led the Packers into the playoffs, but they lost to the Dallas Cowboys in the second round.

Before the beginning of the 1995 season, Green Bay traded Brunell to the Jacksonville Jaguars. There was no longer

any doubt who the Packers' quarterback would be. Favre then had the best year of any Green Bay quarterback in history. He threw a team record 38 touchdown passes as the Packers went 11–5 and won the Central Division of the National Football Conference. Favre led Green Bay to playoff victories over both Atlanta and San Francisco, the defending Super Bowl champion. Against the 49ers, Favre completed 15 of his first 16 passes. He wound up 21 for 28, for 299 yards and two touchdowns. Green Bay won 27–17.

The next week, however, the Packers lost to Dallas 38–27 in the NFC championship game. It was the third straight year the Cowboys had knocked Green Bay out of the playoffs. On the plane ride home after the Dallas game, Favre and other Packer stars vowed to get to the Super Bowl and win it the following season. But Favre almost didn't make it to the 1996 season. In

February 1996, he had surgery to remove bone spurs and bone chips from his left ankle. During the surgery, he had a seizure. Doctors later determined that the seizure could have been caused by the painkillers Favre was taking all the time.

Favre felt he needed the painkillers. After all, the ankle surgery was his fifth operation in six years. But Favre had become addicted to the painkillers. Before the 1996 season, he spent six and a half weeks receiving treatment for his addiction. Then, in July, Favre's best friend, Mark Haverty, was killed in a car accident. Favre's brother Scott was driving the car Haverty was in. Amazingly, Favre didn't let any of this affect his play. He had even a better season in 1996 than in 1995, breaking his team record by throwing 39 TD passes. The Packers finished 13–3. Then they beat San Francisco and Carolina in the playoffs to reach the Super Bowl.

After the 1996 season, Favre became only the second person to be named NFL Player of the Year two years in a row. The other was a quarterback named Joe Montana. "He's the best player in the National Football League," Green Bay General Manager Ron Wolf said about Brett Favre. "He's an amazing player." It was Wolf who made the trade in 1992 that brought Favre to Green Bay from Atlanta. In the third game of the 1992 season, Favre came off the bench and threw a TD pass with 13 seconds left, to give the Packers the victory. He has started every Packer game since. And now he is a Super Bowl champion.